I was told(*):

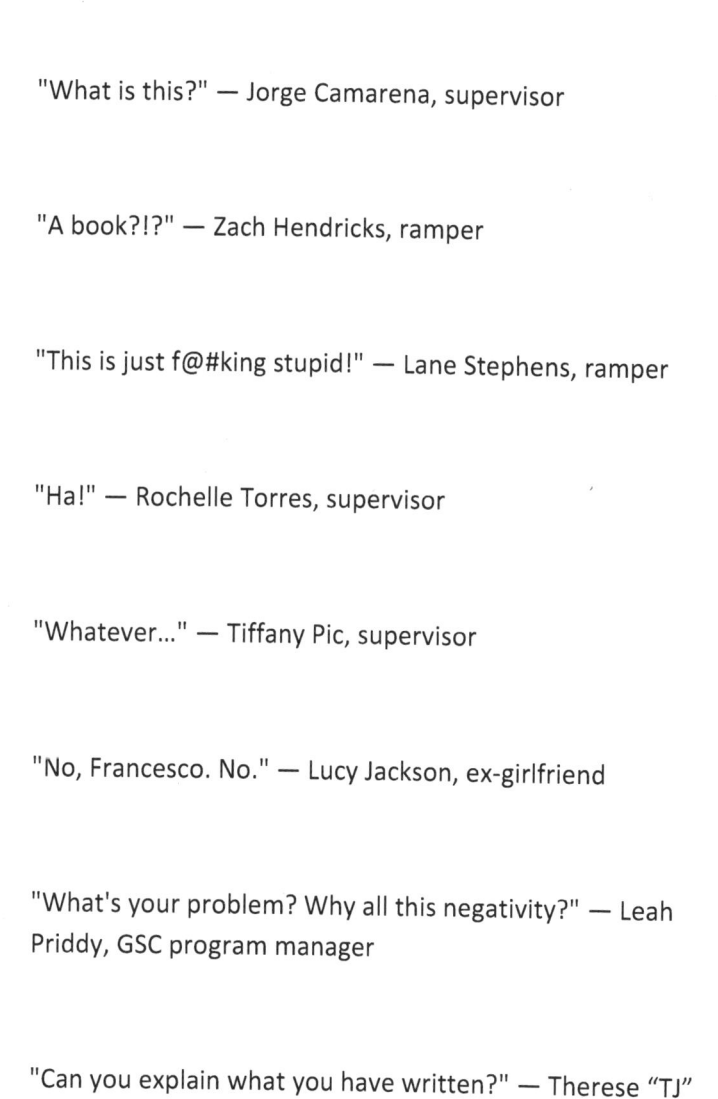

"What is this?" — Jorge Camarena, supervisor

"A book?!?" — Zach Hendricks, ramper

"This is just f@#king stupid!" — Lane Stephens, ramper

"Ha!" — Rochelle Torres, supervisor

"Whatever..." — Tiffany Pic, supervisor

"No, Francesco. No." — Lucy Jackson, ex-girlfriend

"What's your problem? Why all this negativity?" — Leah Priddy, GSC program manager

"Can you explain what you have written?" — Therese "TJ" Grosskopft, station manager

"I think communism is illegal in this country." — Chris Henderson, station manager

"There was no need to talk about strike." — Roy Gourley, station manager

"We take your report seriously" — Barbara Russell, HR manager

"You don't know the possible legal consequences of this." — Mark Zeiger, lawyer

"Not a laughing matter." — Kyle "Pumba" Newcomb, supervisor

"Why all Italians are hot headed?" — Smantha Canavan, ramper

"Why are you so abrasive?" — Liberato Montoya, ramper

"You clearly have anger-management problems." — Amy Dubinsky, ex-wife

"*Sta' tento, che' i te manda a casa!*" — My Aunt Silvana Mauro

"You are a funny little man." — Cindy Jo Turkal, airport agent

"I don't know, saucy Italian..." — Blair Gladwin, airport agent

"You were my favorite." — Kim Kotrch Carter, airport agent

"You are pretty... but I'm taken." — Christopher Clark-Smith, ramper

"*Se almanco te andassi 'n cesa!*" — Mia mamma.

"I agree with everything you have written." — David Meggers, ramper

"My wife said 'we need to invite this guy over for dinner.'" — Gregory Leytem, ramper

"Why do I have to pay for this?" — Ben Martin, ramper

"I don't buy stuff online." — Marita Pence, airport agent

"Hey, these are more than 101!" — Shannon Castillo, ramper

"[long and incomprehensible]" — Kambale "Bob" Mafuta, ramper

"Thank you." — Scott Ramson, ramper

[(*) Not necessarily in reference to this book.]

101 THINGS
A RAMPER SHOULD KNOW
and will never find written elsewhere

by
Francesco Dalla Vecchia

Text copyright © 2018 Francesco Dalla Vecchia
All rights reserved

To Cindy Bohlken

ACKNOWLEDGMENTS

Thank you very much to Gregory Leytem and Wesley Shirley for proofreading my draft.
(All the mistakes left are my fault.)

INTRODUCTION

A ramper is somebody who ramps on the ramp. I am sure that you have seen through the porthole of your plane a guy going around with a high-visibility vest. That's a ramper: an airport agent in charge of loading, unloading, parking, towing, pushing, de-icing and servicing planes. Your trip depends heavily on the ground crew as well as the flight crew. It is not just your bag that they handle: rampers are in charge of your plane during ground operations. Their job is physical, their schedule is terrible, they work outdoors in almost any conditions, and they get paid nuts. If they could strike, they would stop this country, but American laws on transportation have made almost impossible for them to protect their rights (airlines are known for lobbying hard). This book is meant to celebrate their stamina (or craziness).

The tarmac is a playground where rampers are supposed to follow strict game rules. FAA and Company procedures regulate airport operations strictly for safety's and security's sake. Airport agents are required to keep constantly updated, and their training is practically never over. Yet they cannot learn everything from a computer screen or their On the Job Trainer. Experience does it.

I wrote this unauthorized handbook the day I submitted my two-week notice. It literally took me no more than a dozen of hours to complete its draft, and it will not take you more than twenty minutes to read it. My intent was to share what I learned during my experience on the tarmac. I wanted to provide to my coworkers, to airports' new hires, and to everybody who may be interested, a couple of suggestions that hopefully they will find useful. Needless to say, I hope readers will find my style entertaining as well.[1]

You will not find this information written elsewhere for reasons that will soon appear obvious. Admittedly, my point of view is not exactly Catholic when compared with what airlines are preaching. In fact, I wonder if I will ever be able to get another job in the airline industry after publishing this. But, alas, well-behaved rampers rarely make history, no?

---

[1] FYI, these are not "things" and they are not "101." (Every writer is a liar and I want to become one…) The correct term would be "aphorisms," but I preferred to use… an English word in my title.

101 THINGS
A RAMPER SHOULD KNOW
and will never find written elsewhere

SAFETY IS *NOT* No.1. Life comes first... Then happiness, health, fun, etc. We are not here just to survive.

THE LESS YOU WORK, THE MORE I HAVE TO. You are not "stealing from the company," you are screwing my life (see No.1).

THE No. 1 QUALITY OF A GOOD RAMPER IS FLEXIBILITY. Irregular operations happen regularly.

WHEN IN DOUBT, WIN THE WAR. No one complains when planes and bags are on time.

DON'T RAMP if you are afraid of bags.

BAGS DON'T BITE. They kill you slowly.

RAMP LIKE YOU MEAN IT. Being a ramper is like practicing a sport. You get your team, your goals, your challenges, and your score. You need to be fit, a team player, have situation awareness, and especially... have fun playing.

ERRARE HUMANUM EST, PERSEVERARE is what we do for a living.[2]

TREAT ALL PASSENGERS LIKE THEY WERE KIDS. They don't know what's going on. All they know is what they want. It's your duty—as a human being—to teach them reality is not always accommodating.

PROCEDURES ARE EQUAL FOR ALL, but we all have our own style.

WHAT MATTERS IS SHAREHOLDERS AND PASSENGERS. Once you made these people happy... you will be awarded with the possibility of continuing doing it for them.

---

[2] "To make a mistake is human, but to keep doing it… [is diabolical.]" Old Latin adagio attributed to Seneca.

IN CASE YOU WONDER, NOT SHOWING UP IS WORSE THAN BEING LATE. They don't pay me more to work your part, and I tend to be vindictive so... watch out!

IT GOES BOTH WAYS. You must do the right thing, otherwise you are going to be disciplined by those who stand above you. Yet, it is *your* duty to keep your bosses honest as well: never put up with an abuse.

PRAXEOLOGY. If you cannot say something nice about your coworkers, you should probably leave.

IT'S ALL ABOUT COMMUNICATION. The best team is that in which no one has to tell the others what to do.

SHUT UP AND LET 'EM LEARN. Don't lecture the rookies. Let them do it, and they will learn.

THERE IS NO HONOR IN BEING EXPLOITED. Corporations are not exploiting us because they are bad: they are just doing their job. Corporations exploit us because WE ARE BAD: we let them do it to us.

STOP COMPLAINING. No one likes complainers. If you think something can be fixed or improved, say something productive or... ZIP IT!

DON'T WASTE TIME WITH FLIGHT ATTENDANTS. They think you are a loser who works in the dirt; they are like servers looking down at the dishwashers. Pilots know better and they usually treat you like you were human, but don't expect to go to bed with any of them either.

ANYONE CAN PUT BAGS ON A BELT LOADER, but can you pick the best next bag to load so that your buddy in the cargo bin does not have to break his back?

A GOOD PACE IS BETTER THAN A FAST ONE. You save time by being smart. You wear yourself and all the others out when you rush.

PRETTY IS GOOD. If your stack of bags looks neat, you made life easier for everyone.

I WORK FOR THIS COMPANY, NOT THE NIGHT CREW. I don't want to start my shift doing what they were supposed to have done at the end of theirs.

THERE IS ONLY ONE THING WORSE THAN A NIGHT CREW: A *SATURDAY* NIGHT CREW. Beware of Sunday mornings.

TAKE THE DOOR literally. The most important communications your boss has for you are going to be on the breakroom door. It will be written in all caps with no date nor initials and they will all look the same.

COLLECT MONEY FOR SOMETHING anytime the Regional Managers or their friends are stopping by. They love to pull out cash from their own wallets, and chip in for your actual, practical needs (like a new toaster?)

YOU ARE NOT WORKING FOR THE MONEY. You are working for your buddies.

THIS IS YOUR FAMILY. You are going to spend more time with us than with your actual relatives. You did not pick us, and we come in all colors.

WE ALL HAVE OUR DAYS. There's nothing like loading bags to flare down.

DON'T LIE. There are cameras everywhere.

DON'T YELL OR CURSE. Unless you are working next to an engine and somebody is telling you to do something utterly stupid just to establish their authority.

LOW WAGES? They get what they pay for.

YOU ARE EACH OTHER'S ENTERTAINER. Let your friends go home with a funny story to tell.

THE SKY IS UNLIMITED. Working outdoors is a blessing. No matter what, don't miss the show the sky above puts up for you every day.

"*IL SOLE MANGIA LE ORE.*"[3] The most precious thing we have is time. Bet your best time on something worthy.

COMPUTERS ARE APPLIANCES. There is nothing like sitting in front of the computer to appear to be working. Unless your computer is not working.

---

[3] "The sun is consuming your hours." Italian saying.

KEEP THE ENGINE RUNNING next to my nostrils and you will make my life shorter. I'd rather smoke.

RESTROOMS ARE NOT SHIT-PROOF. There is nothing like going to the restroom to make a plane appear on the horizon.

REMEMBER WE WORK AT A STUPID TIME. Brain farts are SBD.[4]

FLIGHT BENEFITS ARE A TRAP. Taking days off to see the world means you are gonna spend money while you are not making any. Consider hitchhiking.

SILENCE IS THE POLITICAL STATEMENT OF LOSERS. Remember to declare independence.

IF ONLY WE COULD MASSAGE EACH OTHER... we would stop from imagining each other naked.

---

[4] SBD: Silent But Deadly.

RELAX. DON'T DO IT. There is always at least one attractive coworker who stirs your blood. But what is more memorable: an unforgettable night of passion, or the awkwardness of meeting everyday afterwards? Perhaps it's better never to find out.

USE YOUR IMMAGINATION to figure out the next thing to do.

IT IS ALL ABOUT LOGISTICS. Aviation is a science based on laws of physics. Most prominently, Murphy's Law.

ENERGY DRINKS MAKE ME WORK BUT THERE ARE CONSEQUENCES. It costs me money working here. Angry.

ALWAYS WEAR PPE IN THE BREAKROOM.[5] Eating in the breakroom is less hygienic than dumping airplane waste. Get your vaccinations up to date.

INFORMATION IS POWER. Not sharing information is as harmful as using it to maintain dominance.

---

[5] PPE: Personal Protective Equipment, such as gloves, googles, etc.

THE TARMAC IS A MANLY WORLD, but we guys have our own periods.

COFFEE IS FOR THE BRAVE. If you can drink airplane coffee, use brake oil as chaser.

STEALING FROM A LOCKER MAKES YOU SUBHUMAN. You shouldn't be here. I mean. On this planet.

STRETCH BEFORE LIFTING. Yeah! Stretch your imagination and find a better job!

DON'T QUESTION AUTHORITY. Annoy authority. Less effort. More results.

THE BEST FORM OF PROTEST IS... Follow procedures by the book. And no plane will be on time.

ENJOY YOUR FREEDOM. There is nothing like working outdoors next to a jet engine while everybody is wearing hearing protection if you need to fart really badly.

SOME QUESTIONS ARE BETTER NEVER BE ASKED, like "why are all TSA officers overweight?"[6]

WAKE UP. If a player waits for his coach to tell him what to do, he will always be late.

ALWAYS DISPLAY YOUR SIDA BADGE,[7] unless the weather is bad. I have never been challenged on the tarmac when it was pouring, freezing, or just a bit miserable.

EARPLUGS WILL NOT SAVE YOU from the crap you will hear today.

IF IT LOOKS CLEAN, IT IS CLEAN. Hence it doesn't need to be cleaned.

"WHO ARE YOU?" IS NOT A RHETORICAL QUESTION. When a passenger asks for a preferential treatment, ask them why they think they should be treated differently from the others?

---

[6] TSA: Transportation Security Administration
[7] SIDA: Security Identification Display Area is the part of the airport in which agents are required to have an ID badge displayed at all time.

IT IS NEVER THE COMPANY'S FAULT. Two jobs, double shifts, early start, working late, 60 hours per week, sleep deprivation, faulty equipment, scarce organization, shorthanded, lack of experience because of the constant turnover, whatever... when you damage a plane it's never because THEY put a $50 million piece of equipment in the hand of a guy who works for 9 bucks per hour.

DON'T WORRY ABOUT DAMAGING AIRPLANES. The worst that may happen to you is that you could be forced to find a better job... as some form of punishment.

FREE TEES FOR EVERYBODY. Anytime a manager gives you a free t-shirt with the company logo/motto, just ask them to put one on, take a pic, and post it on the social media for the amusement of the masses. Truth is: they never wear what they pick for you to put on...

DO THE RIGHT THING: pay us more: at least the equivalent of minimum wages adjusted to inflation. It's a matter of decency.

EVERYTHING WE BRING TO WORK MAKES OUR COWORKERS FAT: donuts, cupcakes, cookies, BD cakes, etc.

THE WORST PASSENGERS HAVE A HUGE SENSE OF ENTITLEMENT. Our patience has a price. Ask for a tip or even a bribe.

PEOPLE MUST UNDERSTAND that the airport is a developing (part of your) country.

HANDLING BAGS IS GONNA MAKE YOUR SKIN THICKER. Wear gloves to save the softness of your touch for your beloved.

FLY INTERNATIONAL TO CATCH UP WITH THE LATEST BLOCKBUSTERS. With your flight benefits a transoceanic flight costs less than a movie ticket and you get to watch at least three features films (and three more coming back).

FIGHT FOR YOUR RIGHTS. If you don't, who will?

DON'T BE AFRAID OF LOSING WHEN YOU FIGHT FOR RESPECT. Fighting is what makes you a better person regardless of any possible outcome.

YOU GO TO WAR WITH THE ARMY YOU HAVE. Human resources are like GSE: they are limited and getting older.[8]

PETS ARE NICE but don't feel obligated to feed the rodents and cockroaches that call the breakroom "home"

ON THE TARMAC TALK LIKE IT WAS A COMBAT ZONE. We will have time to chit-chat later.

POSE SIMPLE YES/NO QUESTIONS to check your understanding.

FOR F@#K'S SAKE! JUST SAY "YES" OR "NO" before telling me the entire story of your stupid life as an answer!

DON'T USE PRONOUNS OR ELLIPSIS OVER THE RADIO. What does "I don't see them here" mean? Are you talking about passengers or bags? Agents or tags? And where the heck is "here"? What in the world do you want me to do now?

---

[8] GSE: Ground Support Equipment, such as tractors, carts, pushtugs, beltloaders, de-icing tracks etc.

IGNORANT MANAGERS FROM TEXAS CALL YOUR CRITICAL THINKING "NEGATIVITY" because you are positively demonstrating their points to be wrong.

THE MICROWAVE IS FOR FOOD ONLY. I tried to dry my socks but I almost set the fire alarm off...

DON'T WASTE MONEY ON FANCY GLOVES. They will break soon. If you don't lose them first.

DON'T BITE YOUR NAILS after servicing the lav.[9]

BRING NON-ALCHOLIC BEER TO THE NEXT STATION POTLUCK just to make your manager nervous.

BE NICE WITH THE GATE AGENTS: they may have to rebook 130 people today.

YOU WILL NEVER LEARN A FOREIGN LANGUAGE ON THE RAMP, but you may grow to appreciate many funny accents and peculiar expressions.

---

[9] "Lav" is short for "lavatory."

MACHISMO WANTED. You may have lifted 1.5 tons of bags today with your guns, but I'll see your virility only when you will stand up for your rights and fight corporative exploitation.

"I DON'T GIVE A F@#K"? There is always something you care about. That's what defines you.

AIRPORT AGENTS ARE SOCIAL ANIMALS. Nothing is more rewarding than spending time with your friend coworkers outside work. Play some sport, travel, hang out and have fun with them. It will make work and your whole life taste better.

ON THE TARMAC IS LIKE IN THE SOCCER FIELD: you need to be in the right place at the right moment, otherwise...

CALCULATE THE COST OF WHAT YOU ARE WEARING. Steel-toe boots, $85; longjohns, $8; overall/sky pants, $24; gloves, $14; balaclava, $12; etc. It's expensive to work here, isn't it?

WE TAKE CARE OF OUR OWN. 4, 6, 8, 13 eyes are always better than 2. Let's look after each other.

SCANNERS ARE SCAMS. The next time somebody wants to explain to you how a scanner works, have them put on two pairs of gloves, get into the restaurant freezer, and ask them to type on the screen while you are pouring water over their head and blasting hard rock music into their ears. It's only fair.

22 INCHES ARE NOT THE SAME FOR EVERYBODY. For some non-rare carryons, entitlement makes 22 inches longer. Since when measures don't matter anymore?

DON'T TOLERATE PHOTOSHOPPED IMAGES OF YOUR COMPANY. I saw posters bragging about the quality of the company people in which employees were represented by models/tokens. Evidently our best workers don't look pretty enough.

MANDATORY SHIFTS ARE THE MEANEST PUNISHMENTS: management should reserve them only for well-deserving rascals.

THE FIRST IS FOR THE GAS. THE SECOND FOR THE FOOD. Sometime later during your third HOUR you finally start to make money (for your rent, etc.)

A MEETING WITHOUT MINUTES IS WORSE THAN A MATCH IN WHICH NOBODY KEEPS THE SCORE. You also save time by sharing an agenda in advance, and read propositions that have been written down beforehand. (The Bocce Club of my parish seems to be more organized than your station meetings.)

FROM THE DEICING BUCKET THE WORLD REVEALS A DIFFERENT BEAUTY. Don't forget to take bird-eye pics of your friends.

DON'T UNDERESTIMATE THE VALUE OF PET THERAPY. Petting friendly pets in transit is as good for them as it is for us.

I DON'T KNOW WHAT IT MEANS when my Philippine friend says "that dog looks good."

THE BEST RAMPERS SING AND DANCE ON THE TARMAC as if they were in the shower. Try to get their medications.

TREAT EVERY SINGLE BAG AS IF IT BELONGED TO A STRANGER, because in most of the cases it does.

GIVE A DETERGENT BOTTLE AND A RAG TO A NEW HIRE AND SEND HIM TO THE COCKPIT TO WIPE CLEAN THE REARVIEW MIRROR, and he will learn never to trust you again.

ULTRAVIOLET RAYS ALWAYS GET UNDER YOUR SKIN even when it is cloudy. Beware of exposure to sunburned rampers.

THEY KEEP TELLING YOU TO STAY HYDRATED, but drinking is not allowed on the tarmac.

"*COSA FATTA, CAPO HA.*" An already accomplished task is one less to do later.

WHAT GOES AROUND, COMES AROUND. Most belts end in a loop.

FRAGILE? There SHOULD be no fragile bags. There COULD be insured bags, but they WOULD not...

SHIFT TRADE IS BUSINESS AS USUAL: there are winners and losers. Get over it.

EXPAND YOUR HORIZONS. TDY is the ultimate way to explore new cultures... and learn to challenge your certainties.[10]

SOME BOSSES THINK THEY KNOW EVERYTHING even before hearing what happened. Make sure they get the whole picture before they take their decisions.

IT IS NOT A CONTEXT between you and my Pet Rock®. When was the last time you admitted to be wrong?

TEAMWORK is so that we can share responsibilities. It's never just one person's fault.

IMPERATIVES ARE FOR BITCHING. Questions are kind. Ask "can you help me?" If you don't want to be hated.

THE COMPANY WANTS TO HEAR YOUR CONCERNS, get as much information as possible, and prevent you from suing them.

---

[10] TDY: Temporary Duty Yonder, or the deployment of airport agents to help short-handed airports.

"THIS IS NOT A COURT"—my boss once told me—"You cannot plead the fifth." Apparently your constitutional rights are suspended once you sign up for the ramp.

THE ROLE OF REPRESENTATIVES WITHIN THE CORPORATION IS THE SAME OF A SUGGESTION BOX. No leverage equals impotence. (I bet your representative is floppy too.)

MANAGERS HAVE THE RIGHT TO IGNORE YOUR REQUESTS, instead of replying with a "no" and explaining why. You have the right to call that "disrespect."

PLEASE AND THANK YOU. I allow my friends to skip that. I hate my foes for skipping that.

DOT-MATRIX PRINTERS ARE THE REAL TERRORISTIC THREAT. It's like somebody was still trying to shape their life according to a primitive piece of fictional literature belonging to an extinct tribe of more than 2000 years ago... Only Reason will set us all free.

ASSERTIVENESS means not having to ask: "Why didn't you tell me?"

NO ONE GETS IT. If you want to drive your managers mad during a meeting, tell them you are "seeing something and saying something."

WAITING ON HOLD DURING A CALL TO YOUR INSURANCE COMPANY AIN'T THAT BAD after spending long hours in the bagroom without music.

A RAMPER WITHOUT A CATCH PHRASE is a paper puppet.

RELATIVITY. When pushing the position of the tow bar is more important than that of the push tug.

BE ON INTIMATE TERMS WITH EVERY PIECE OF EQUIPMENT. They all have their idiosyncrasies.

HORSEPLAY IS A MUST for kids to develop skills and fitness, muscles and bones. When will you ever learn to control a tug on the snow if you don't skid? To drive over a cone if you don't try? To jump over a tow bar if you can't lift your knees? To keep your balance when somebody is moving up or down the beltloader conveyer? Better get some practice and be prepared.

A SUPERVISOR MUST BE A PROBLEM SOLVER, not a problem maker.

THE HARDEST JOB AT THE AIRPORT is making the weekly schedule. They try to make everyone happy, but everybody is gonna be unhappy no matter what. How about a requiem for the HR?

OBSERVING GOOD WORKERS IS A GREAT WAY TO LEARN. You can stare and nobody will complain for your voyeurism.

IT IS OK TO STOP THE CHATTERBOX during the station meeting through the infodesk interphone.

THE DE-ICE TRACK BUCKET IS LIKE A VENETIAN GONDOLA: to stand safely you must always bend your knees a bit. And remember that passengers watching through the portholes rely on you for their entertainment.

THE LOST AND FOUND BOOKS collected at the airport make the worst library ever.

TRAVEL WITH YOUR SIDA BADGE, and then ask concessions a discount for airport workers.

DON'T FORGET SOUVENIRS. You travel somewhere and your buddies cover your shifts: bring something back for them, maybe just the bar of soap from your hotel... but something, please!

THE GOOD, THE BAD, AND THE UGLY. Every station has a pretty one who is unbeatable in avoiding any hard labor, and a couple of heroes who go far and beyond their duties. Don't expect justice.

PUT ALL THE LAZY PEOPLE TOGETHER when setting teams. So that they will learn how it is dealing with people like themselves.

MEDIOCRITY IS EVERYWHERE. You can always absolve yourself.

NO ROOM FOR CREATIVITY ON THE TARMAC, unless you have to solve a *new* problem. And in that case you are going to receive a verbal warning afterwards.

NOW THAT YOU HAVE LEARNED THIS JOB, THINK IF YOU CAN DO IT BETTER. Online training is never over, and neither is perfection. Can you do it quicker? smoother? smarter?

THE BEST REWARD THE COMPANY CAN GIVE TO THE EMPLOYEE OF THE MONTH IS TIME OFF. But they are more likely to hand out a fitness watch.

A NO-NONSENSE LEADER IS A BLESSING. Thank your best masters by giving them the least problems as possible.

NICE PEOPLE MAKE A NICE STATION. A nice place to work is priceless. And it's everybody's responsibility.

AIRPORTS GAVE ME SOME OF MY BEST FRIENDS. I met great people here. And I'm so thankful.

WE RUN THIS PLACE. Without station agents... shareholders and passengers would be totally screwed.

I KNOW NO ALTERNATIVE TO THE UNION. No one can bring improvements without leverage. Only the Union has some. The rest is *blah blah blah* (aka crap excuses to chicken out of conflicts).

I MIGHT BE WRONG. Unions don't fix everything. There are many more solutions out there. Find yours, get something done, and then brag about it: we are all too eager to hear things have finally got better. One way or another.

ANY PROTEST IS A FORM OF PERTURBATION, the rest is just socializing.

"STRIKE" IS THE ULTIMATE F-WORD for Airlines. What are they doing to keep you so polite?

WHAT DID YOU DO? To make this place better than the way you found it? Is there any good reason why you should be remembered?

All safety procedures can be summed up in one line: DON'T BE A MORON!

MORE?

If you think there are more "things" a ramper should know, please submit your contribution to: francesco.dallavecchia@gmail.com

Thank you.

FRANCESCO DALLA VECCHIA [there is no middle name] has been a ramper from 2012 to 2018. He worked for three different airline companies in six different airports, as he was sometimes sent in temporary deployment (called "TDY") to short-handed airports throughout the country. In 2015 he was fired by Envoy Airline Inc. (former American Eagle Airline) after promoting the CWA Union at the company headquarters in Irving, TX. He is currently writing a book on the abuses he endured.

cover picture credit:
that.stormtrooper.guy — Instagram ®

Made in the USA
Lexington, KY
15 July 2018